AF486153

unbroken
SPIRIT

Charleston, SC
www.PalmettoPublishing.com

Unbroken Spirit
Copyright © 2023 by Sheilah Pemberton

All rights reserved

No portion of this book may be reproduced, stored
in a retrieval system, or transmitted in any form by any
means—electronic, mechanical, photocopy,
recording, or other—except for brief quotations in
printed reviews, without prior permission of the author.

Hardcover ISBN: 979-8-8229-1823-8
Paperback ISBN: 979-8-8229-1824-5

Sheilah Pemberton

unbroken SPIRIT

Legacy of Courage

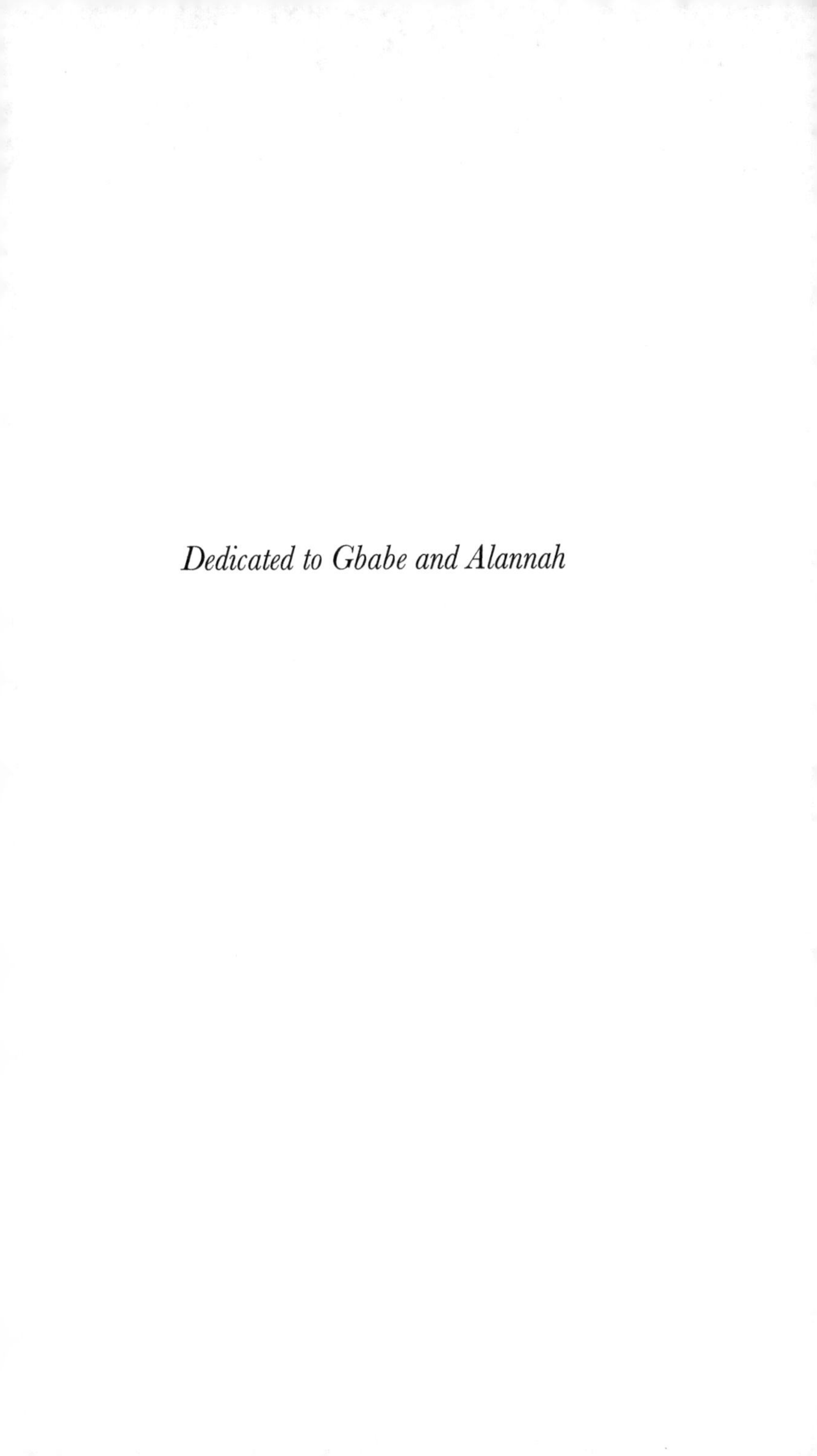

Dedicated to Gbabe and Alannah

If there's a book that you want to read, but it hasn't been written yet, then you must write it.
—Toni Morrison

There is no greater agony than bearing an untold story inside you.
—Maya Angelou

Table of Contents

Yellow Cottage, last remaining original structure. Built around 1885. Original home of the State Home and School for Dependent and Neglected Children

One of the largest impetuses in the foundation of the Rhode
Island State Home and School

part
ONE

History of Orphanages in Rhode Island

Children were often indentured by the state school to commercial farmers. When no longer needed, they were returned to the Rhode Island State Home and School. This began in the early nineteenth century (the 1800s).

These children came from broken homes, or homes where one parent had passed and the other was unable or unwilling to care for the child.

The State Home and School for Dependent and Neglected Children was Rhode Island's first state home for needy children. Established in 1884, it ran until 1979.

State Home and School Asylum Projects in Rhode Island
established in 1884

rare childhood photo of the Pemberton siblings, 1954

Chapter One

Mount St. Francis Orphanage

I don't really have memories of Tiverton, Rhode Island, or living at home. I have seen pictures of myself with my brothers and sisters, but my earliest memory is the day my fraternal twin sister (Cyndi), brother (Gregory), and I were told we were going on a ride into the country.

I remember being excited and jumping in the back seat. Auntie Phillipe and the auntie from Westport were in the front. Cyndi was wedged in between Gregory and me in the back.

As I looked back, I saw my mother standing in the doorway. I smiled and waved, but she didn't. Little did I know I would see her one more time, and after that I would see her in a coffin. I was also about to discover a word known as terror. I would come to feel it many times.

I must have dozed off, because I opened my eyes to the car slowing down. We were in front of a large, gloomy-looking brick building: Mount St. Francis Orphanage, my new home, although I didn't realize it then. We slowly got out of the car, and it immediately took off. I turned to see Gregory running after the car, yelling for the aunties to come back. A man in some sort of work clothes ran and brought Gregory back up the drive.

Slowly I realized they had left us there and were not coming back. Cyndi began to cry. Gregory and I surrounded her as we saw two nuns approaching us with stern looks on their faces. Yanking my hand out of my brother's, one snatched him and took him in one direction, while the other commanded me and Cyndi to follow her. Gregory was taken in through another door. We were led into a large hall with beds positioned close together. "You will sleep here for now. We will find something permanent later." The word *permanent* resounded in my head.

> *"When my father and mother forsake me, then the*
> *Lord will take me up."*
>
> —Psalm 27:10

Later that day we were lined up and led to a huge dining room for dinner. Spotting Gregory, I broke out of the line and raced over to hug him. I was stopped by a sharp pain in the back. One of the sisters had hit me hard. "You will never break the line again or go anywhere without permission! Do I make myself clear?" I looked toward Gregory, who signaled me to be strong by lifting his chin with his hand. Nodding in agreement, I went back to my place in the line.

The next morning, we were taken to the hair shop (as it was called). Our ponytails were cut off without ever being taken out of the band. Now I was crying. We suddenly had no hair. A slap quieted me quickly as we were told, "No one has time to be doing this kind of hair around here!"

In the orphanage the Sisters of Mercy, who were nuns, were cruel and strict and had no compunction about beating the daylights out of me. It was known as discipline. It was here I first learned how to scrub on my hands and knees. I learned to hide my feelings and became what they wanted: quiet and submissive. However, this didn't always work, as my rebellious nature sometimes took over. Rebellion had no place here. Cyndi was spared the beatings. She was small, fair-skinned, and petite. I was often beaten for some imagined slight or oversight.

Discipline was a word I would come to hear over and over. Being dark-skinned and only one of three "Negro" orphans (as we were called), I was fair game for abuse and taunts. Blackie, ugly, monkey, and nigger were often used for my name. I downplayed my intelligence in the classroom. I stayed in the shadows, kept to myself, and tried to make myself small. I found comfort in walks in the woods surrounding the orphanage. I also found I loved water.

Mt. St. Francis had a large pool. I couldn't swim yet but loved to sit there. I often watched the white kids swimming, wanting to swim as well.

We were allowed to swim once they had tired. I didn't really like it too much, knowing the others had deliberately peed in the water. Soon I had learned to be sneaky. I could easily get out, go to the pool, and try to learn how to swim on my own. Not a good idea, as I was caught the third time out.

What I did learn to do was write I MUST OBEY on loose-leaf paper, front and back. I often dreamed that my mother would magically appear to take us all back home. A dream I held on to, and it often helped me get through the worst of times when I was so lonely.

> *"I can do all things through Christ which strengtheneth me."*
>
> —Philippians 4:13

St. Aloysius Orphanage

Former residence of Saint Aloysius Orphanage, now
Overbrook Academy

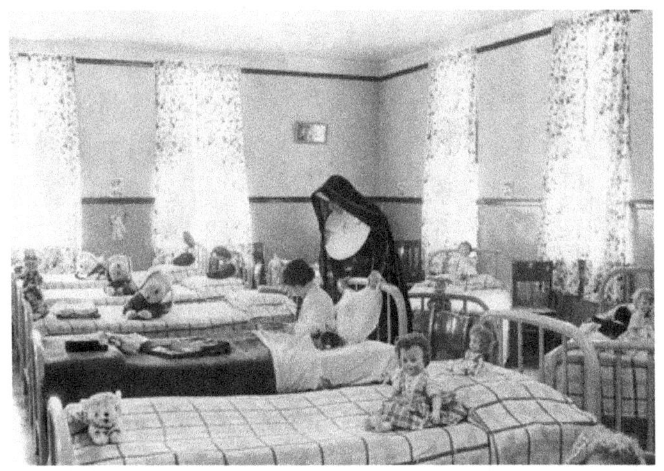

Standard orphanage dormitory, Saint Aloysius

We were only five when we were transferred. My brother had "aged out." Seeing that our family had been split so much, they wanted to keep us three together. I still held on to the dream of my mother coming to get us.

We went with Gregory. Our new home became St. Aloysius Orphanage. This new orphanage brought with it more discipline and much stricter rules. We now had a big dormitory, which housed about twenty or more beds. They were in rows with an aisle straight down the middle. That aisle had a significance that I would come to know and dread all too much.

Lights out signaled bedtime. The first night there, I asked if I could sleep with Cyndi. Sister Blandena said no and that we would learn to sleep in our own beds. We were given these ugly, creepy-looking dolls whose eyes continuously stared at me. She put Cyndi far away from me, closer to where she slept in a walled-in room of the dormitory. Sighing, I told Cyndi I was right across the room if she needed me. I wondered how Gregory was doing. Although in the same orphanage, he was alone in the boys' dorm. I at least had Cyndi.

It was still dark. I wondered why we were getting up and ordered to stand beside our beds. Five o'clock became the start of our long day. After bed check, panty check (to ensure we hadn't wet the bed), and group showers, we were taken to the dining room for breakfast. I caught sight of Gregory but knew not to run to him.

Life was hard at such a young age. I learned to avoid eye contact with the nuns. I also realized that obedience often brought its own rewards. Sisters of Mercy, they all were called, although I didn't experience any mercy. It was hard being so different from the other girls, who were all white with pretty hair in various shades and eye colors. I stood out even from my twin sister, who was short, fair-skinned, and petite like a little doll. I was tall, gangly, and often told that I was ugly.

The white girls always made fun of my short hair, which made me look like a boy. It sat on my head like a wool cap. I didn't know how to comb my hair, as it was always cut off once it started to grow. I was constantly punished for not doing a chore fast enough. Their favorite was always a hard slap across my face.

Cyndi was punished in other ways. Once when she couldn't finish her food, her head was forcefully held underwater. Father Guertin, the orphanage chaplain, took a particular interest in Cyndi. I would sometimes see him taking her to a small building. I realized later it was a shed where tools and supplies were kept.

I remember asking her why she got special treatment from Father Guertin, since he seemed to basically hate me. She didn't answer that question. After a while she became quiet and wouldn't talk, but she was never too far away from me.

It wasn't until much later that I would know what had happened to her.

* * *

Months turned into years, and I did what I was told to maintain peace. The chores were endless. Sister Blandena took particular pleasure in my polishing the "middle aisle," which had to be done on hands and knees using a special thick paste called beeswax. I waxed until she could see her face on the dark linoleum floor.

One day after much pleading, I was convinced to play a game of dodgeball with one of the girls. It was a game where you threw the ball against the wall and the kids behind you would dodge it. Unfortunately, the girl I played with didn't dodge quickly enough and the ball hit her in the mouth, knocking out her front tooth.

Screaming, she ran inside and told a sister I had hit her in the mouth. When the sister came outside, she had a look on her face that told me to brace myself for punishment. Grabbing me by my ear, she marched me upstairs to Sister Augusta. This sister dished out what was then called corporal punishment.

One really didn't want to be sent to her. She proceeded to beat me with a wide leather strap with slivers that stuck out. I raised my arm, trying to stop her from hitting me in the face. My right arm still bears a six-inch scar, faded now but still visible. After a while I felt myself slipping into a quiet kind of darkness. I heard a voice from far away telling Sister Augusta that was enough and to stop.

It was there and then, at that early age, I learned not to cry—to stand strong and silent, which I found out enraged the sisters even more. They were continuously determined to break my spirit.

After my time in the infirmary, I knew that I wouldn't play with any of the other girls ever again. Cyndi was my only comfort then. I rarely saw Gregory, which hurt my heart, to be in the same place and not be able to talk to him. I occasionally saw him through a chain-link fence. All I could do was link my fingers through the fence as a way of saying hello.

One of the few joys I had was roller skating. In the orphanage's basement was a huge hall with concrete floors, and we could roller skate down there. I became somewhat of a recluse. I didn't form friendships, nor did I want to.

Chapter Three

Funerals

One day in late summer, Cyndi, Gregory, and I were picked up by a social worker. She took us to a green house in New Bedford, Massachusetts. It was the home of my family. We were six years old at the time. Dropping us off, she told us she'd be back in a few days to pick us up. It turned out that my older sister Elaine had been killed in a fiery car crash at the age of fifteen.

I remember the first thing that caught my attention was the black drape hanging across the front door.

I later learned that this was a traditional way of letting neighbors know there was a death in that particular house. Once inside we were greeted by my mother and siblings.

I remained quiet because I still didn't know them. Also, the atmosphere in the house felt like a dark cloud permeated every room. It was a house of sadness. I also saw a big grandfather clock that had a cover over the face. I didn't know the reason for covering it, although I heard later that the clock was stopped and covered at the time of death.

The biggest shock for me came when I saw a coffin in the living room, with flowers on each side of it.

We were taken upstairs with the second set of twins, Beverly and Colleen. They were younger by two years.

Later that night the house was very quiet with everyone asleep. I snuck out of bed and crept downstairs. I felt myself being pulled toward the living room. My heart was pounding in fear, but I was determined to see what or who was inside the coffin. As I stood there trying to get the courage to follow through, I heard a sound behind me. My heart jumped, but I saw it was my older brother Kenny. He was sitting quietly in a rocking chair. I could tell he'd been crying.

He motioned me to come to him. I sat on his lap, and he rocked the chair, never saying a word. I felt a strange sense of peace and security sitting there. He never spoke one word, just rocked and stroked my hair. I awoke the next morning in bed next to Cyndi.

The remaining days passed in a blur, then we were taken back to the orphanage. Life resumed like this had never happened. My mom and siblings stayed in the back of my mind. I kept wondering why we couldn't live at home. We had a mother and father. We were not orphans, so why were we even here?

So many questions with no answers. Years passed and life became routine.

* * *

One bright August day, Sister Blandena told us we were going on a trip to the beach (if we completed our chores). I happily did all the chores, excited not only at the prospect of going to the beach, but also of seeing Gregory. The girls were isolated from the boys, so I had little opportunity to actually talk to him.

As we lined up to get on the buses, I noticed the tone and mood of the sisters had changed. They were being nice and spoke softly to us. Once on the bus, I noticed Gregory was not there. Hesitantly, I raised my hand and asked for him. I was told he was sick with bronchitis and would not be coming. They omitted his true illness and hospitalization.

The beach was called Horseneck. I instantly fell in love with the ocean. Here I could feel the wind on my face and felt free. Smelling the air and salt water stirred something in my soul.

I heard my name being called, so I reluctantly ran to where Cyndi was. Father Guertin said he had something to tell us. "Your mother passed away this morning," were his next words.

Not understanding, I asked him, "Where did she go?" I looked at Cyndi, wondering why she was crying so hard.

"She went to heaven to live with God," he said. Now I understood.

I stood frozen on the spot as my sister attempted to grab and hug me. I shrugged her off. That day the nine-year-old child I was disappeared. (Even though I was not then aware of it.) I knew without a doubt now that my mother would never come to get us, and I felt anger building up inside of me. Silently, we boarded the bus to go back. I sat quietly, holding Cyndi's hand.

Looking out the window, I noticed we were going in a different direction. Suddenly, the bus pulled up to a green house at Four Thirty-six Purchase Street. Standing out front was a group of people. I remembered them. They were my brothers and sisters, older now, as was I. Once again, the black cloth draped the front door.

Father Guertin swung open the bus door and told us we could get off. One boy ran up and hugged us, saying he was our brother Warren. We were allowed to stay there through the days leading up to my mother's funeral. Gregory joined us the next day. I saw my father, who seemed like a shadow. He rarely spoke and he kept to himself. Kenny was inconsolable and retreated somewhere after punching a hole in a wall.

Those days were confusing and filled with a new kind of despair. I found myself talking less and thinking more. I wanted to cry and could feel the tears in my throat, but they wouldn't come, so I swallowed them and kept my head up.

I met so many relatives during those days and realized I had a very large family.

Seeing my mother in her coffin, her final resting place, was the hardest pain inside thus far. She looked so beautiful and seemed to be merely sleeping. On the day of the funeral, two black limos pulled up to the house. All the girls rode in one with my father. Gerri, Cyndi, Colleen, Beverly, and myself. In the other were Sonny, Joe, Jimmy, Kenny, Bobby, Warren, and Gregory.

Afterward the hopeful thought I had was that we would get to stay with family. There were so many cousins, aunts, uncles, as well as sisters and brothers who were all grown up.

The one thing I will never understand is why we were made to return to the orphanage. No one stepped forward to take us, not even my father. He'd barely looked at me or spoken to me anyway. I sensed anger, as well as his sadness.

We returned to St. Aloysius. Life went back to hard work and discipline.

Chapter Four

Mrs. Tavares

By early September we were called into Mother Superior's office. When Cyndi and I arrived, Gregory was already there. He had a determined look on his face. Puzzled, I stood silent. There was a very large black woman dressed in black, sitting in a chair. Very large because I could only see her and not the chair itself.

As we stood there, I realized from her words that she wanted to take my brother to live with her. She stated she didn't want any girls. "Girls are trouble," she said. I heard Mother Superior tell her that Gregory would not go anywhere without his sisters. "They've been split enough as a family. Their family does not want them split up."

Our family? I scoffed inside. What a joke. Anger still simmered inside of me, although I kept it well hidden. We were out of the orphanage now. I realized it was because

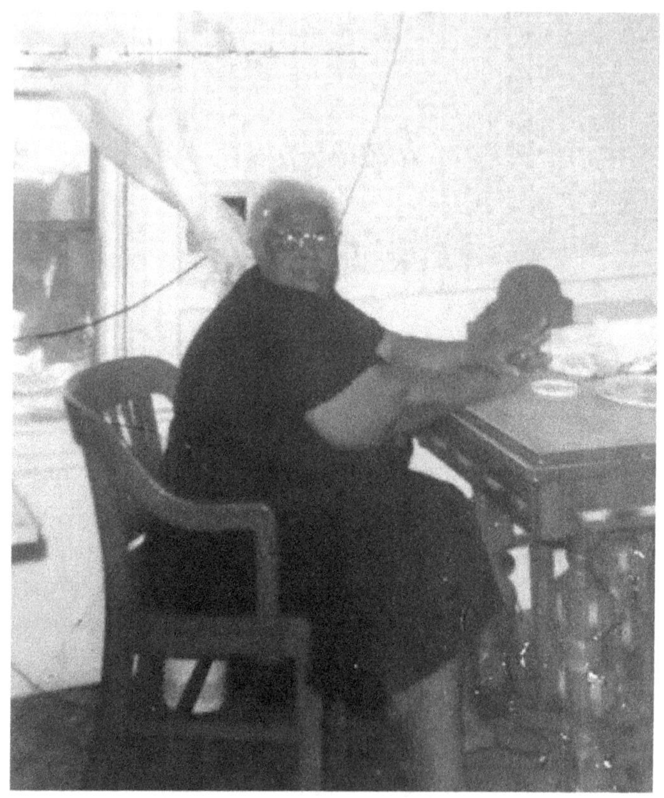

Mrs. Tavares

my mother was dead, which meant we could be fostered out or adopted.

Within a week we left with Mrs. Tavares—the three of us. The new house was a big, gray three-story building located in Providence, Rhode Island. Thirty Cypress Street became our new home.

Life changed for us once we were in foster care. We were registered in a private Catholic school called Holy Name. For the first time, I made friends. Linda Lopes became my best friend. She lived directly across the street from me, and we walked to school together. Linda was the first friend I ever had. She was the same color as me and I found that so comforting.

The first thing Mrs. Tavares did was send us to a hairdresser, who washed and used a hot comb on our hair.

I was so happy to see I could now comb my hair or brush it back.

Home life was still very strict for me and my siblings. We were used to scrubbing floors and woodwork, and we were always the last to eat because we had to serve all the other people (adults) first.

Mrs. Tavares used to be a nanny who took care of the "rich" children in the East Side Blackstone Blvd. neighborhood. They would sometimes come to visit her, which I hated. She would make us serve them and wait on them when they wanted lunch or something to drink. We were given their leftover clothes.

She did allow me to hang out with Linda a lot. We both got bikes and would ride everywhere together. Linda didn't seem to mind my acting like a boy. I often heard her comment it was safe that way.

Linda decided one day to take me on an early birthday adventure. We were both fifteen and full of mischief. Linda had moved from across the street, but we were still inseparable. She wouldn't tell me where we were going, only to make sure I got a good night's sleep. She told me to pack sandwiches and that she would bring the Twinkies and Kool-Aid in her thermos. I had a hard time sleeping the night before, but I was up early that morning. I did all my chores as fast as I could. Mrs. Tavares was in a decent mood and was allowing me out for the day.

Securing my peanut butter and jelly sandwiches on the back of my bike, I raced outside. We'd agreed to meet at the Cypress Street playground. Linda was already there, waiting. We both wore blue jeans and sweatshirts. It was a warm and beautiful spring day in April. We rode our bikes along Camp Street, and we chattered all the way there before she would tell me anything.

We were going to have to sneak in to where we were going. "Don't worry, it's perfectly safe," she said.

We biked up to Brown University. Walking our bikes through some underbrush, we hid the bikes and grabbed our stuff. I followed her to a brick building and pried open the side door. It was dark and kind of musty. We went upstairs to an old, seldom-used balcony that was filled with broken chairs and cobwebs.

I whispered my fear of spiders and rats. Linda laughed and reassured me no rats but didn't mention spiders.

There was a nice space to crouch down, and I realized we were in a hall at the university. Safely hidden, I could see, between the balcony slats, the large hall below was filling up.

When I gave Linda a questioning look, she merely put her finger to her lips. I shrugged and wondered what this great adventure was. Suddenly, the murmuring below stopped and it became very quiet.

A man began to speak. I didn't know who he was but knew I'd heard that voice before. I was about to experience my adventure.

Peeking over, I observed a black man of medium build. Glancing at Linda with a frown, I whispered that I was not interested in some boring speech.

Martin Luther King, Jr., began to speak. I became totally enthralled with what he was saying. His voice was quite familiar, yet powerful. My mind didn't know exactly what he was saying, but I recognized the words racism and inequality. Dr. King spoke of the war in Vietnam and about civil rights.

In my innocence about world affairs, I didn't understand everything he was saying, but I listened intently and noticed the tears glistening in Linda's eyes. Something shifted inside of me. I knew instinctively I was listening to history being made.

Riding home, the chatter was absent. We both were quiet, each occupied with our own thoughts. It came to my mind where I had heard that voice before. It was on television. I was eleven years old at the time. Four little girls had been killed in a church bombing, and I remembered the adults talked about little else at the time. I thanked my friend for the adventure.

Mrs. Tavares had taken in more foster children. All boys, from the age of three to nine. I was charged with taking care of them. Once, little Harold jumped out of the tub where I was trying to give him his nightly bath. He ran naked into the living room where Mrs. Tavares was entertaining some guests. Laughing, I ran after him.

The guests saw the humor in it. She, however, did not. After I had gotten Harold settled for the night, she called me into the living room.

She then backhanded me and ripped the whole front of my dress off in front of the guests, asking me if I thought that was funny. I ran from the room, totally humiliated. I did, however, get back at her. I had to scrub her under-clothes on a scrub board in the tub after I put the rest of the little ones to bed. I took a pair of her underwear, which was extra big. Rebelliously, I wrung it out and took it into the living room, stretched it out as far as I could, and asked her if she thought they were clean enough.

I wanted to ask her if she thought that was funny but held my tongue, enjoying her embarrassment.

The guests, being uncomfortable, made their excuses and left. I was always the punching bag for her. I made her even angrier because I wouldn't cry. I heard her comment that she would break my spirit if it was the last thing she did. I angrily thought if the nuns did not break my spirit, she wasn't going to.

She seemed to get angrier because I was developing breasts. I was growing up, and not to her liking at all.

We lived in a boarding house. The first two floors were three-bedroom apartments. Big rooms. A living room, dining room, hallway, kitchen, pantry, as well as three bedrooms. The second floor was rented out to a family. The third floor housed separate rooms, with a kitchen and bathroom for the boarders. Mrs. Tavares took in many immigrants from Cape Verde and Portugal. Our job was to clean the rooms up there, as well as the first floor.

Gregory had a room upstairs as well. I spent a lot of time with him, reading comic books and talking. I was so happy to finally be around him. We became exceptionally close as I was a total tomboy, and we even had a paper route together. We made money in the winter, shoveling snow. We were like brothers. Although no matter how much I wished otherwise, I was still a girl. He taught me how to fold the papers and throw them just right to land on the porches. I followed him everywhere, even playing football. He taught me how to ride a bike. He was always so patient with me. We were like two peas in a pod. As I got older, Gregory wouldn't let me play ball with him anymore. Having matured much too quickly to my liking, the boys were beginning to take notice. A fact I hated. He gently explained to me why and that he would always look out for me. I understood and we became closer. We developed an unspoken bond that no one would ever be able to break. It exists unspoken to this day.

part TWO

Chapter Five

Jimmy Duarte

Mrs. Tavares had an adult son, Jimmy, who drank quite a bit. We slept in her room on a cot. At nine years old, we were so innocent with no knowledge of the evil to come. At least for Cyndi. Jimmy used to come into the room at night through the bathroom, which was off the kitchen and led to Mrs. Tavares's room. He would just sit on the edge of the cot, rubbing our feet. His presence was uncomfortable. Once I told Mrs. Tavares, she put a lock on the inside of the bathroom door, which stopped him from coming into the room.

One Saturday, Cyndi and I were cleaning the third floor. My "foster brother" Jimmy lived on the third floor in one of the rooms. Girls were only allowed up there to clean and hang clothes from the third-floor window. (Except for me when I was hanging with Gregory.) I hated to go into Jimmy's room. It smelled of stale cigarettes, nasty beer, and alcohol. Assuming he was not there, we went in to clean his room. I had my obligatory clothespin on my nose.

Jimmy, however, was in the room. He motioned us to the bed, stating he was a doctor and needed to examine us. As he sat on the edge of the bed, he instructed us to pull our shorts down so he could examine us. Even at the age of thirteen, my gut flipped and I told Cyndi to leave. I fled downstairs, assuming she was right behind me. She wasn't.

As I slowly climbed back up to the third floor with dread, I heard Cyndi coming down the stairs. She had a strange look on her face. When I asked her what was wrong, she slowly shook her head and said not a word. She never went back up to the third floor. I was afraid to mention the incident as I thought we'd be sent back to the orphanage. I tried to pretend that everything was okay. Did Mrs. Tavares know her son was a child molester? I think back and realize she must have. It was why she didn't want any girls. Cyndi was not the same after that. She told me that she would always love me, but she became quieter and sullener. I saw her changing but couldn't help her. She wouldn't talk to me. Not then anyway. Cyndi grew more and more discontent and quiet.

She ran away a year later at the age of fourteen.

Chapter Six

Sweet Sixteen

By this time, I had my own room with the mandatory lock on the inside of my bedroom door. Which meant I was able to lock myself in each night. This eventually worked to my advantage. I was able to sneak out at night. I would wait until I heard Mrs. Tavares snoring, then off I'd go. By this time, my sister had her own apartment in Chad Brown Housing Projects and a baby girl named after me, Lil Sheila. I would always make it back before it was too late and got away with it all the time.

I had grown tired of Catholic school with its rigid rules and regulations. Not to mention the nuns and their strict codes. Linda had moved away from Cypress Street, but we still hung out together. I became so depressed about wanting out of Catholic school, I began to rebel and did everything I could to get out. I had my eye on going to public school. After enough rebellious behavior, I was sent to Nathan Bishop Junior High. I loved it. I met a new friend named Myso Bright. She was smart, funny, and so easy to talk to. I brought her to my house one day after school, and I was pleasantly surprised to see that Mrs. Tavares liked her. We became inseparable after that. A friendship developed between us that lasted until her death, forty years later.

Nathan Bishop was like a whole new world for me. Gone were the rigid Catholic school rules. Being a teenager was fun and exciting. Unfortunately, it also left me open to a negative element, one I was inexplicably drawn to. I didn't let it interfere with my school attendance or classes, but the Chad Brown gang from junior high hung out exactly where I snuck out to.

As my sixteenth birthday approached, I had no way of knowing the disaster that was coming.

Myso, who came regularly to my house (and I to hers), got together with Mrs. Tavares, who decided to throw me a sweet sixteen surprise birthday party. Because it was a surprise, Myso didn't consult me on the guest list. She had no way of knowing the "gang" I hung with would cause such chaos.

On the day of the party, I was feeling down because my twin sister once again was not there to celebrate our birthday together. Mrs. Tavares sent me out for a walk. I did become pleasantly surprised with the surprise party, until I saw the guests who yelled, "SURPRISE!" Instead of presents, they had brought Ripple and Boone's Farm. They poured them all into the punch bowl. Then they went into Mrs. Tavares's room and started rummaging, lighting up reefer, and making out with their girlfriends. Myso and I were terrified and asked them to leave. We knew all hell was going to break loose.

Mrs. Tavares hit the roof and managed to kick them all out, including Myso. I fiercely defended her as she didn't know they would act like idiots. I consoled Myso, who was in tears, and told her not to worry and that it would be fine. My sixteenth birthday ended up with a strap across my back and increased restrictions.

One of the outlets I enjoyed, was the part-time job that I got at sixteen at Miriam Hospital. My job title was called "tray girl" working in the dietary department. It was then I recognized the first stirrings of the satisfaction I received helping the sick and helpless.

I was able to buy clothes I liked and stopped wearing my hair in braids, but rather wore it out, letting it hang close to my shoulders. Mrs. Tavares opened a savings account for me. Of course, it was a joint account, with her being the primary. Still, I had my own allowance. I began going to the Young Men's Christian Association (YMCA or Y) after work. I only worked from 4 p.m. to 7 p.m.

Springtime brought more daylight hours. I was growing up. I had been wondering why my heart would pound at the sight of this boy I saw constantly at the Y. I had to at least find out his name. I sat on a bench and waited, my heart pounding. I saw him walking toward me and could hardly breathe. Just as he reached me, someone called his name. Bruce! He turned to answer them and then walked toward them. I wasn't disappointed, however. I had learned his name. I knew I would see him again.

Other than my job, I was still restricted at home. If there were any football games I wanted to go to, I would simply stay out and not go back home after school.

The restrictions brought more rebellion on my part. I began to rage against the servitude, which increased daily for me. It was school, home, cook, serve, and home-work. No extracurricular activities like cheerleading or even going to basketball games at Central High. I missed Gregory but knew he was busy with football and getting ready for college. Happy for him, even though he was never home.

Summer came and I was happy to be out of school. Myso and I had gone to Casual Corner, a popular store in the city. She helped me pick out some cute summer outfits.

One day Myso and I went up to the Y. It was a nice summer day. I had taken the time with my appearance and wore white shorts with matching sandals and a green tank top. I had my hair in a big, perfectly rounded afro that I was extremely proud of. I had confided in Myso about my feelings, and she laughingly said it was my first real crush. Maybe she was right, but I had to find out for myself. I sent her to the store as I saw the group approaching the basketball court.

Disappointment was on my face as I realized he wasn't with the group of boys playing ball. Sitting quietly, I heard movement behind me. My heart started pounding before I even turned around. I knew it was him. He spoke my name out loud and said hello. I turned and met his eyes, and my heart was pounding so loud, I was sure he could hear it. He sat on the bench next to me and started a conversation. I asked him how he'd known my name and what his name was. (Like I didn't already know.) I couldn't take my eyes away from his hands. They were big yet soft looking. I wanted to touch them but didn't dare.

Being near him did things to me I truly didn't understand and had no intention of sharing with Myso.

I saw her coming from a distance and rose to meet her. I told him, "See you later," and he reached for my hand and kissed me on the cheek. I left, smiling over my shoulder at him. As I walked away, I could feel him staring at me but did not turn around. My heart, however, was singing. We met often that summer right there at the Y basketball court. We used to go to the Strand Theater downtown and sneak in the side door to watch movies. We talked and laughed, and my first kiss on that dark balcony in the theater was like a dream.

There were always girls around the guys at the Y. Prettier and much more experienced. The girls teased me a lot about still being a virgin. Bruce, however, wasn't interested in them. I never told him about my feelings and each time an opportunity came, I kept silent. He didn't keep silent, however, and told me he wanted me to be his girl.

I didn't think I was pretty, nor did I feel I could compete with the other girls. Bruce was so kind and caring. He respected my "virgin status." He told me that was what made me different.

My first heartbreak came in a way I never saw coming. He didn't leave me for another girl. Bruce had been drafted into the army. I was totally devastated, as was he. There wasn't anything we could do about it.

The summer had ended, and I became immersed in my studies at school. Always in the back of my mind was Bruce, my first crush, whom I had convinced myself was my first love. I didn't hear from him right away, as he was in boot camp, basic training that would last for nine or ten weeks.

I couldn't wait for Thanksgiving when I knew he would be coming home on leave. When he did come back, I was amazed. Bruce the boy was gone and in his place was a very mature man.

He was home for fourteen days. When he told me he was shipping out to Vietnam, I cried like a baby. We spent as much time as we could together, going for walks in the park and talking about a future together. There was no longer a doubt in my mind or heart; Bruce was my first true love. We promised to write, and my young sixteen-year-old heart promised to wait for him. After he left, I tried my best to stay happy and lived for his letters. They always came to Myso's house. Mrs. Tavares would not have understood or given me the letters.

His younger brother Chris found me just after Valentine's Day and broke the news to me that he had been killed in Vietnam.

I felt betrayed and felt the pain of heartache as well, knowing I'd never see him again. With that loss came a whole different attitude. I was angry and resentful. I still went to school, but it was all different.

Chapter Seven

Runaway

The final straw for me at home came one day when I returned from school. By this time, it was just me. Gregory had gone off to college, Boston University. For some reason, Mrs. Tavares was in a foul mood. She started yelling at me the moment I came through the door, ordering me to go clean my dresser drawers. They were already clean, but I took them all out and refolded them neatly. I also rehung all my clothes in the closet.

When I was finished, she came in and threw all the clothes on the floor from both the dresser and the closet, telling me to do it again. She then slapped me so hard across the face, my neck snapped back. Her two-hundred-plus pounds put everything in that slap. Besides my neck, something inside me snapped as well. I had had enough. I began yelling at her, telling her she wasn't my real mother and I had done everything she'd ever asked of me. She laughed at me and told me my real mother hadn't wanted me to begin with, that I was lucky she had taken me in. "Lucky?" I asked. I laughed back at her, and then told her the true words I couldn't take back. "Your alcoholic son raped my sister and drove her out of here. Now I'm out as well! You will never hit me again, never again!!!" With that I slammed out and left her standing there, speechless.

I ran away from home that day and headed straight to Myso's house. I stayed there for two weeks, continuing school.

I knew, however, that I couldn't stay there indefinitely because I was still technically a ward of the state. Cyndi couldn't let me stay with her. Even though she was an emancipated grown-up, I was not.

My social worker was waiting outside of my school one day. She told me she'd found me a new foster home. Despite all my savings and clothes, I had bought over the months working, Mrs. Tavares transferred it all into her bank account and wouldn't allow me to come get my clothes.

What she didn't know was that Myso had stashed quite a bit of my earnings for me, so I was able to go buy a lot of new clothes. My new foster home was on the South Side, the Clements family. It was a large family, and Mrs. Clements also had foster children.

She was so different from my previous foster mother. She was kind and funny and had a southern accent that I found enjoyable to listen to. She had four adult daughters. They were so nice and all so pretty. I had a lot of fun listening to them.

I was able to stay in the same junior high school and still hang out with Myso. I didn't have to sneak out anymore. Mrs. Clements gave me so much more freedom. As long as I did my chores and took my turn cooking.

I knew I would age out of the foster care system within a year when I turned eighteen. I learned a lot about southern cooking and Ma Clements taught me how to make Southern fried chicken. I still spent a lot of time with Myso. For the first time, I was able to go to sports events at school and didn't mind my ten o'clock curfew.

I still went back to visit "Ma Tavares" on Cypress Street. Once I didn't live there, we were able to communicate better. She acknowledged her son's part in my sister's leaving her home. I think she always knew, and it explained why she'd never wanted girls in the first place.

She also admitted Gregory had always been her favorite (after her own adult son, that is). Years later on her death bed, it was Gregory's name and face she remembered and wanted to see, despite her dementia.

I learned that forgiving her was going to benefit me. She no longer had a hold on me. Now I didn't mind helping her and went to see her often. The other foster kids had all either grown up or gone somewhere else. She was now too old and didn't have the energy for kids anymore.

What pleasantly surprised me was that whenever I visited her and she had company, she'd always brag and say, "This is my daughter, she's going to be a nurse."

Life went smoothly, and soon I aged out of the foster care system and finished school.

Myso left home and moved to New York. She had gotten a job at Bloomingdale's. I was happy for her but so sad to see her go. We promised to always stay in touch, no matter where our lives took us. My friend Linda had succumbed to diabetes.

part
THREE

Chapter Eight

Roy

Soon I got a job working at the Women & Infants Hospital in the family planning department.

I liked the job and learned to counsel teens on birth control. My life was peaceful, and I was learning to be independent. I would go over to my cousin's house in the village and help her do hair. She had a shop in her basement. It was fun for me.

One day I was there, and the most incredibly handsome man came in. He was from Jackson, Tennessee, visiting his brother, a neighbor of my cousin's. When our eyes locked, I thought to myself, "No way, he's too good looking." I immediately felt a dislike for his arrogant nature. Snubbing my nose at him, I said goodbye to my cousin and left.

He, however, must have liked what he saw in me. He began to always be over at my cousin's house. Persistence on his part finally won out. I went on a date with Roy. He was eight years older than me, twenty-six to my eighteen. He was silly and made me laugh. That was the first pull. It wasn't long afterward that he began to occupy my thoughts more than anything else. I found a cute little furnished apartment on the East Side and moved in. Roy had returned to Tennessee, as his mother had become ill and he went home to check on her.

For the first time since Myso left, I experienced loneliness. I continued to work, but at one point, I moved back to Mrs. Tavares's home. It was easier and cheaper, as she didn't charge me rent.

She had gotten older, and I didn't mind looking after her. I had long ago forgiven her.

Roy wrote me long letters, describing the beauty of Tennessee and telling me I should move down there. There were plenty of job opportunities and nursing schools. I was reluctant to move, however; I didn't want to leave Cyndi. I eventually got an apartment in Chad Brown not far from Cyndi.

One day after returning from work, I was surprised to find Roy sitting on my porch. As he hugged me, I noticed the suitcase next to him. Without asking, Roy assumed he could move in with me, which he did. It was okay at first because I was so smitten. He got a job, and everything was great.

Chapter Nine

This Is Not Love

As I draw ever closer to Jesus, I am becoming more receptive to the messages I believe He is sending me. I also realize He and only He blessed me with strength I didn't know I had inside of me. It all centers or at least comes back to the abuse I suffered from the age of four (in the orphanage) and into my years in Jackson/Memphis, Tennessee. Domestic abuse back then was not only acceptable, but also not talked about.

Heads turned away and eyes were blind to the swollen lips, black eyes, and numerous bruises. It wasn't until the broken cheekbone and jaw, which precipitated my accidental overdose, that it came to light.

I opened my eyes, trying to remember where I was and what had happened. The pain in my face and jaw was excruciating.

After I adjusted my eyes to my surroundings, I realized I was in a hospital. But I couldn't, for the life of me, remember how I'd gotten there. Cyndi was sitting by my bed, asleep.

Trying to speak I realized my mouth was wired shut. Panic set in. My monitor began beeping and the nurse came rushing into the room. "Oh, you're awake! You've been asleep for over twenty-four hours. How do you feel? I know you can't answer. The doctor wired your jaw and cheekbone together, they were both broken." Her words came tumbling out of her mouth.

Memory flooded back as I remembered Roy had landed a serious punch to my face in a fit of rage. I had been to the ER previously for a broken nose and had been given Darvon to relieve the pain.

When Roy broke my jaw, I was reluctant to go again to the ER. The pain was so bad, I was taking Darvon every hour to help relieve the pain. I was found by Roy unconscious when he came in. I was told an ambulance took me to the hospital.

Darvon was banned in 2010 by the Food and Drug Administration for its extremely addictive nature. It was also found to have a dangerous effect on the heart due to propoxyphene. The main ingredient found in Darvon was propoxyphene.

Cyndi, who was now awake, explained she had my babies with her, and I was not to worry about anything. Stating she'd be back, she left to make some phone calls.

As I lay in that hospital bed, my mind started rewinding. I should have walked away the first time Roy hit me. Why didn't I? Love? Did I even know what that was? I'd never experienced it growing up, other than Cyndi and Gregory.

Was it because I was beaten from a young age? Did I think that was normal? I just didn't know.

I dozed off, only to awaken with the sounds of sobbing in my ear. Roy sat at my bedside, sobbing like the true coward he was. "I am so sorry, Baby. I don't know what happened. Will you forgive me? Never again, I promise!!!"

What the heck was he crying for? I couldn't speak, and the pain I felt defied description. My finger under the cover pressed the call button. When the nurse hurried in, I signaled her to get my unwelcome visitor away from me. After telling him he had to leave, she gave me the welcome shot of morphine, and I once again drifted off to that blessed sleep.

Drifting back to sleep, I remembered the first time I saw Roy and my initial reaction. He was very handsome, yet I had felt an instant dislike for him. Why hadn't I listened to my gut, and why, even now, was I numb at the thought of him leaving me?

Was I crazy or just stupid?

Little did I know the repercussions of this whole drama would follow me for most of my life. Two months later I was released from the hospital and allowed to go home. Since I insisted, I had slipped on the ice, there wasn't much that could help me out of my situation.

My diet consisted of liquids. Milkshakes, broth, gelatin, and soups became my steady diet for a year. All nutritious but not chewable. Roy tried to be the epitome of the perfect man and doted on me. He even moved us to Jackson, Tennessee. Then the nightmare really began. I was far away from the protection of Gregory.

One might wonder why I went back to a life with Roy. Growing up without a father, I wanted my children to have theirs. I stayed and slowly felt the strong spirit I possessed being subdued deep within me.

Roy would fly off the handle at any given moment. I clearly remember one night (one of so many), I had put his dinner in the oven and went to sleep. I awoke to him loudly calling my name. I got up and went into the kitchen. He had the dinner plate in his hand and asked me what the hell it was. My body stiffened as I knew I wouldn't escape his anger that night. Dumping the plate on the floor, he said it was only fit for dogs to eat. He then shoved me to the floor, demanding that I eat the food.

I managed to run to the bedroom and lock the door. He busted through the door and punched me in the face, breaking my nose. After a final kick in the side, he banged out the door. I prayed so many nights for strength. Not for the strength to endure, but for the strength to escape without killing him. I knew it was not the answer. I prayed for God to return my spirit to be courageous and strong for my children.

That spirit returned when two incidents initiated the turning point. The first incident happened one night when it was late. I could hear his footsteps coming up the porch stairs. Louder and stronger. My hand reached for the knife under my pillowcase, which I kept hidden there, praying all the while that he would not be violent or angry. As the bedroom door opened, I tightened my grip on the knife. Luck was with me that night, as he passed out at the foot of the bed. I realized that I had to get out of that living hell, had to get my life back. I knew that in my heart as I cautiously got up and went to sleep with my babies in their room.

The second incident occurred when one day, Roy's car pulled up and my children both ran, not to him, but to hide. At two and five years of age, they had begun to fear him. He had a girl with him. As he brought her into the house, he introduced her as Terry. My new replacement. I felt an anger I had never felt before. As she sat down on my couch, I was told she was a college student at Lane College. The college was within walking distance from my home.

The duplex I lived in had a water pump in the back-yard. I told Roy I was feeling faint and asked him to get me a glass of water. Surprisingly, he acquiesced.

Once I heard the back door shut, I ran to lock it. Coming back, I released all my anger on Terry as I commenced beating her ass. Not because she now had Roy, but because she had the audacity to set foot in my home with my children. As I kicked her out of the front door, I told her she was welcome to Roy and to remember this when he started to abuse her as well. My last words were, "A tiger never changes his stripes." I heard years later she definitely experienced all that abuse and more.

At this point I didn't care if Roy came at me, I was going to defend myself. I was going to show him he had not broken my spirit. Ironically, he didn't come back in the house, nor return for a month.

I had started to plot Roy's demise; it was time to do something. I had a choice now, kill or be killed. Stay or leave.

One day not long after that incident, I walked down to Big Mama's house (Roy's mother).

We had a good relationship. She had taught me the secret to great-tasting biscuits from scratch. She was the best. I was about to find out how even the best can betray you.

Knocking three times, then coming in was always our signal. When I walked in, there sat Big Mama on the couch, laughing and talking to Terry. I looked into her eyes and saw sadness there. I turned and walked out without a word. It was obvious she had betrayed me. I never went back there.

It was then I began to plan my escape. Saving most of the grocery money allotted to me by Roy, I would buy the cheapest brands of food. I would make meals that would last for at least two days. Roy was usually out drinking or carousing after work, so it was usually just my babies to feed. I had dropped to a hundred pounds.

Slowly, my savings began to increase. I almost had enough to buy a bus ticket. I had it all planned out. I knew I would be able to get to the bus station. My next-door neighbor was a very nice man. We lived in a duplex, so I knew he had heard the violence I endured. He often asked me to come stay with him. I knew that was not the solution to my problem. He agreed to get me to the bus station when the time came, but I couldn't accept his offer to buy my ticket. My time was coming soon enough.

Chapter Ten

Escape

I had left and gone back so many times. I knew I had to be very cautious and plan everything just right to get away. One of the things in my favor was Roy had a rigid work schedule. It kept him out of the house pretty much all day.

In the weeks leading up to executing my plan, I became outwardly submissive. The children were fed and quietly asleep in bed by the time Roy came home. Whatever was going to happen, I had to make sure he didn't become suspicious. What little clothes I planned on taking were packed and next door with my neighbor, who was going to give me a ride to the bus station.

I had convinced Roy that the children needed new coats and shoes. He did buy them these items. I wasn't allowed to purchase clothes for myself or them.

The day finally arrived, and I awoke with a new feeling of hope and determination. Roy left that morning for work, looking at me with a puzzled expression on his face. For a brief moment, I thought he might have figured out what I was planning. He sort of shrugged at my silence and went out of the door with his usual "Have my dinner hot and ready" edict.

Nodding in agreement, I went to the door and watched him leave. Nervously, I waited two hours before venturing next door. The three short knocks signaled my readiness. As I left, I glanced around at the neatness of the home I had made without one feeling of sadness or remorse. I had sandwiches and snacks my neighbor had brought me, and I was ready.

We made it to the bus station without incident. My neighbor gave me his phone number to call when I arrived safely.

We were on the bus when I looked out the window and saw Roy's car approaching. Fear shot through me, but the bus pulled away. He followed it for a bit, honking the horn. I could see the tears in his eyes from the bus window as he rode alongside, yelling my name.

He must have realized I had gotten away because he stopped following the bus. Breathing a sigh of pure relief, I offered a prayer of gratitude to God for allowing me to escape.

To this day I don't know how he figured out that I had left.

What I didn't know was that he would follow me later and show up again in my hometown.

What he didn't know was I had Gregory now and knew I'd be safe. Gregory knew I was coming home.

It was a cold late-February evening when I showed up at Thirty Cypress Street. The home I had once run away from was the sanctuary I came back to. Gregory opened the door to let us in. I saw the angry yet relieved look on his face, but at the time I was too tired to even wonder about it. The twenty-four-hour bus trip had worn me out.

He settled us in my old room, and I, for the first time, felt completely safe and at peace. Sleep for all three of us that night was long and peaceful.

"The Lord is my shepherd; I shall not want."

—Psalm 23:1

"He restoreth my soul."

—Psalm 23:3

Chapter Eleven

Restoration

Life settled peacefully for me. I found that Gregory had been angry at my appearance. My normal 140-pound weight had been reduced to ninety-eight pounds. Not realizing it at the time, I looked like a skeleton.

Time and healthy meals returned my body to a normal, healthy weight. I enrolled my daughter in kindergarten, and she began to thrive.

I moved into my own apartment early that summer. Gregory had gotten me a job at Bannister House, where he worked as a physical therapist. I worked as a nurse's aide. I enjoyed helping people but was not satisfied with the work. I wanted more. I knew then I'd finally be able to go to nursing school. Roy could no longer stop me.

One afternoon I returned home with my children to find Roy sitting on my porch. No suitcase this time, for which I was relieved. Anger, not fear, coursed through me at the sight of him. He stood up and asked if he could come in. I told him no and suddenly my then three-year-old son ran at him, shouting for him to go away. "I hate you!!!" he cried. "Leave my mommy alone!"

The look of shock registered on both our faces. Roy, however, cried and said he would leave and not bother us again.

I told him I had forgiven him. He would always be welcome to contact and be in his children's lives.

An offer he never took me up on. Years later, Roy contacted me and asked for my forgiveness for breaking my jaw and all the abuse. I told him I had forgiven him long ago. We formed a communication and conversed throughout the remaining years.

That night I thanked God for all the blessings He had given me. Strength, courage, resilience, and an unbroken spirit.

Acknowledgments

First and foremost, I want to thank God for blessing me with life and an unbroken spirit.

Many voices encouraged me throughout the twelve years I procrastinated writing this book:

my daughter, Marquetha, for reading through my manuscript, giving me sound advice, and encouraging me never to give up;

my sons, Sabu and Gregory, for their unwavering support;

my sister Cynthia for her acknowledgment that my story had to be told while allowing me to tell part of her own story that intertwined with mine;

my brother Gregory for always being my voice of reason;

My niece Lil Sheila for her humor and insight;

My childhood mentor and friend Emilia Lopes, who gave me unconditional love.

References

DeNoon, Daniel J., "Darvon," November 19, 2010, https://webmd.com/painmanagement/news/20101119/darvon-darvocet-banned/.

Dillon, Hilary, "Yellow Cottage," *Rhode Island Monthly*, November 21, 2012, https://www.rimonthly.com/rhode-island-colleges-yellow-cottage-ribbon-cutting/.

History of Rhode Island Orphanages, https://rhode-tour.org/tours/show/1.

Orphanage, Saint Aloysius; Ignasher, Jim, "A Place to Call Home," November 22, 2014, smithappleby-house.org/a-place-to-call-home/.

Overbrook Academy, formerly Saint Aloysius Orphanage, picture courtesy of www.overbrookacad-emy.org

Soules, Rebecca, "Let Us Build a Home for Such Children," 2003, https://rhodetour.org/items/show/1.

Standard Orphanage Dormitory, Saint Aloysius, November 23, 2018, amilkovi@providencejournal.com

"Wikipedia: Elizabeth Buffum Chace," Wikimedia
    Foundation, last modified March 24, 2023,
    00:02, https://en.wikipedia.org/wiki/
    Elizabeth_Buffum_Chace.

www.ingramcontent.com/pod-product-compliance
Lightning Source LLC
Chambersburg PA
CBHW071949120726
48001CB00005B/2099